God Loves Me

COLORING

~~AND ACTIVITIES~~

BY JB ROBOR

FUN

FOR AGES 5 - 10

God loves YOU!

God Loves Me Coloring and Activities Book

Children's Book, Puzzles

Ages 5-10

ISBN: 9798732801644

Illustrator: Evgenia

Some images from Pixelbay

Bible Verses from KVJ

Celebrate Life

Burlington, North Carolina, USA

www.JBRobor.com

Printed in the United States of America

First Edition

Dedication

Especially for

YOU!!!

This Book Belongs To:

____

BINGO FUN ON THE ROAD

Players: 1 per bingo card
When you see any of the pictures below, put an X
on it. The first person to have a row with 5 X's is a
winner! Row may be diagonal, horizontal, or vertical.

 SPEED LIMIT 55	GIRL		 YIELD	
 STOP	CHURCH		CAR	
		FREE SPACE		
BIKE			TRUCK	
		BOY	 DO NOT ENTER	COW

TIC TAC TOE
Players: 2
One player marks X's; the other player marks O's. Take turns marking your blocks.
A player wins when they have marked 3 blocks in a row, vertically, diagonally, or horizontally.

PLAYER 1
PLAYER 2
PLAYER 1
PLAYER 2

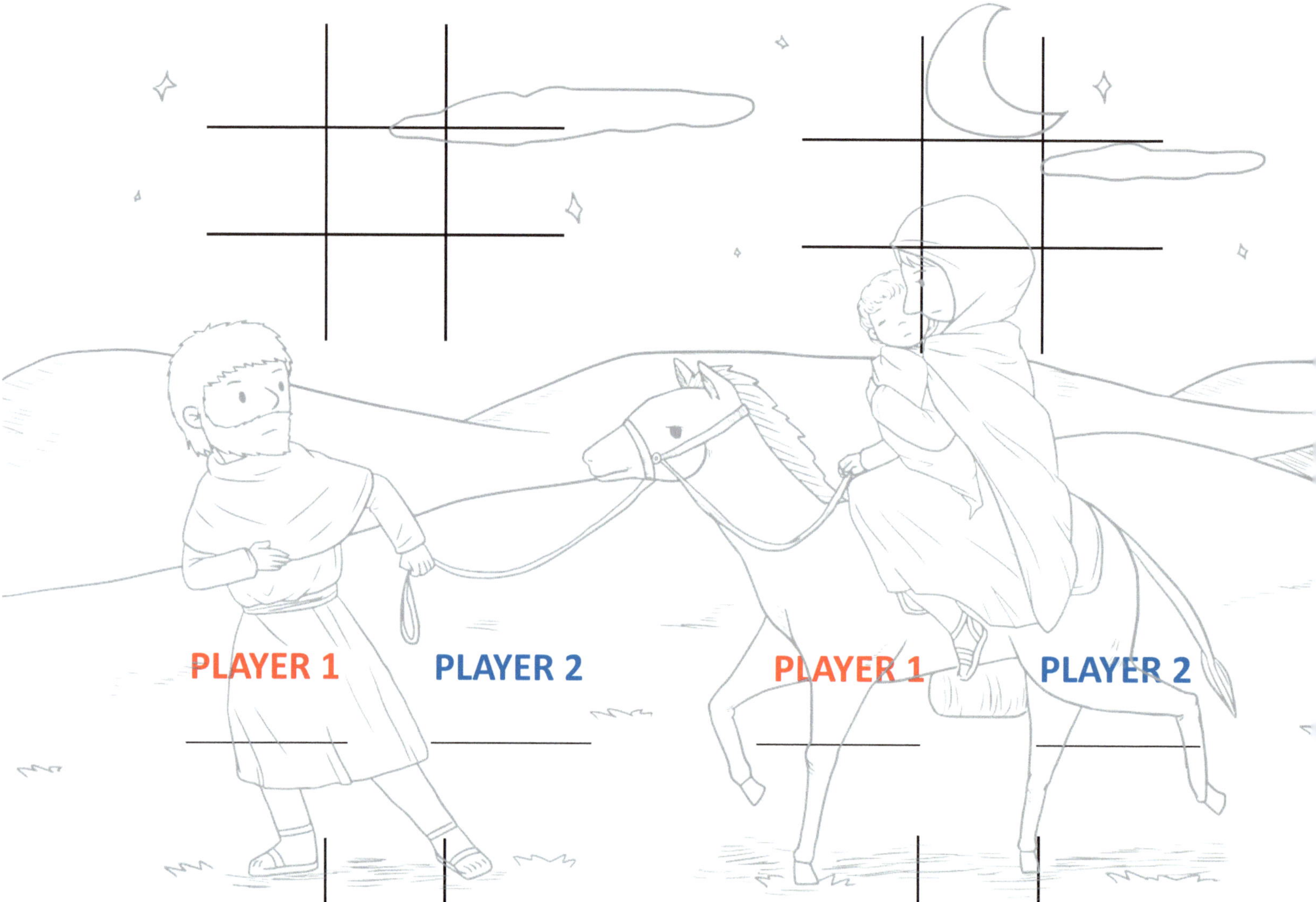

PLAYER 1
PLAYER 2
PLAYER 1
PLAYER 2

JESUS
LOVES
ME
THIS
I
KNOW

MATCHING FUN

ONE	5
TWO	8
THREE	7
FOUR	10
FIVE	3
SIX	9
SEVEN	1
EIGHT	6
NINE	4
TEN	2

BULLS & COWS

Players: 2

One player thinks of a 4-digit number (Example: 1234). The other player tries to guess it by putting a 4-digit number in the Guesses squares (one digit per square). The first player tells the second player how many bulls and cows he has guessed. Bull = correct number in the correct position (Example: 1 in the first position would be a bull). Cow = correct number in an incorrect position. Second player wins if they can guess correctly all four numbers, in correct order, before the end of the grid.

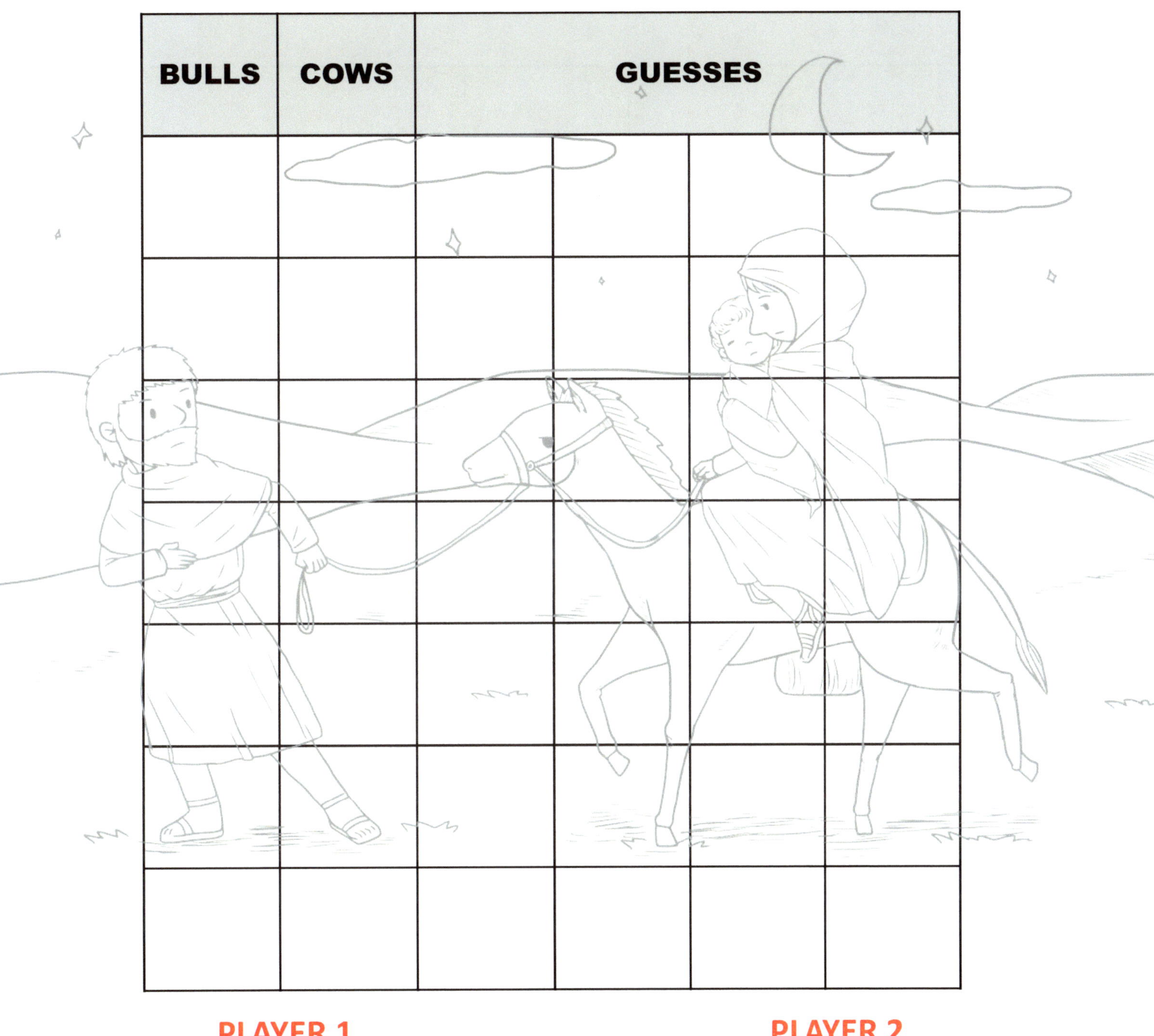

PLAYER 1

PLAYER 2

CONNECT 4 FUN

Players: 2

Each player picks a different color to color their disks. Take turns as you try to build a horizontal, vertical, or diagonal row of 4 while preventing the other player from doing the same.
The first player to connect 4 disks wins!

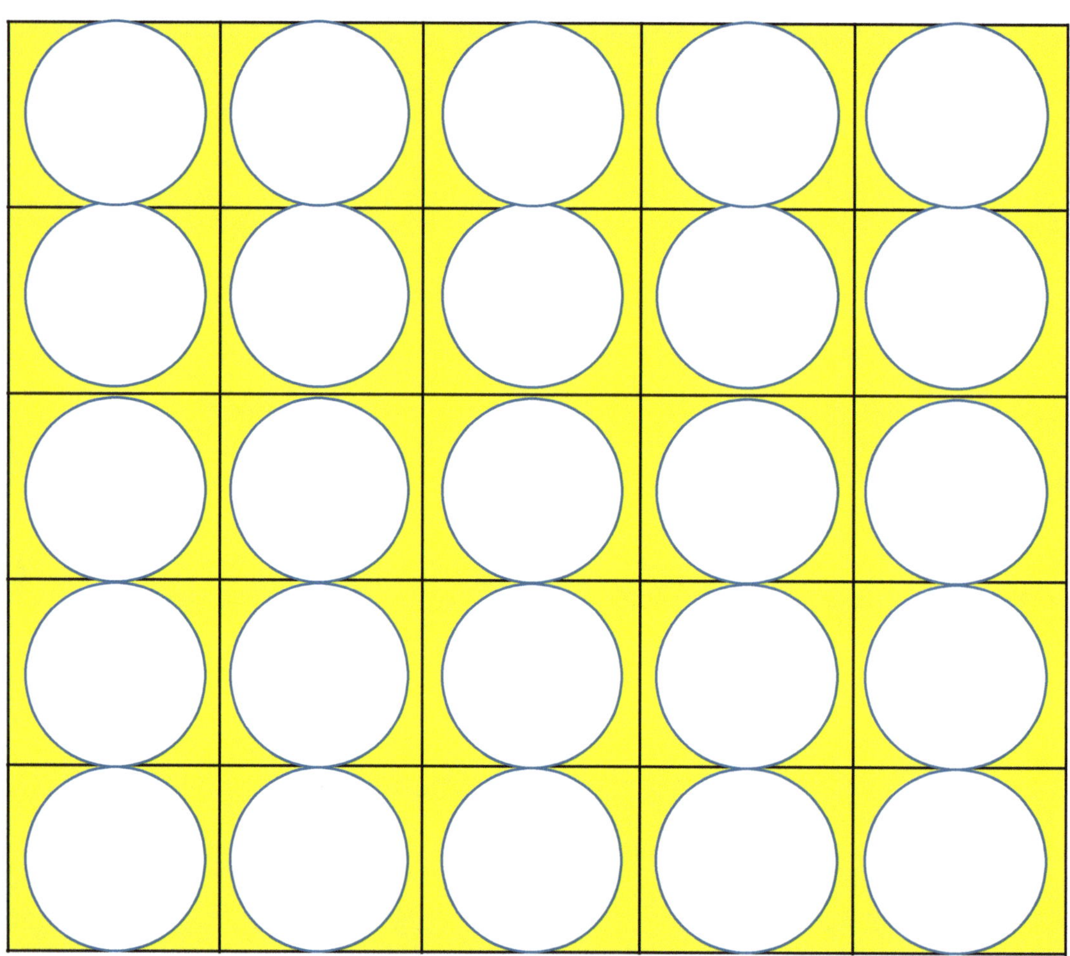

PLAYER 1   **PLAYER 2**

_______________   _______________

BINGO FUN ON THE ROAD

Players: 1 per bingo card

When you see any of the pictures below, put an X on it. The first person to have a row with 5 X's is a winner! Row may be diagonal, horizontal, or vertical.

ROAD				**CHURCH**
	BOY			**BIKE**
SCHOOL		**FREE SPACE**	SPEED LIMIT 55	STOP
TRUCK				**CAR**
	YIELD	**GIRL**		

BLOCK 'EM FUN

Players: 2

One player marks X's; the other player marks O's. Take turns marking your blocks. You cannot mark a block next to the other player's marked block; leave at least one empty block in between. A player wins when the other player has no block left to mark.

PLAYER 1 PLAYER 2

ON YOUR MARKERS

Players: 2
Each player starts by putting a marker on a dot. When both players have put their two markers on
two separate dots, players take turns moving their dots to the empty dot using the lines.
When one player can no longer move their dot, the other player wins the game!

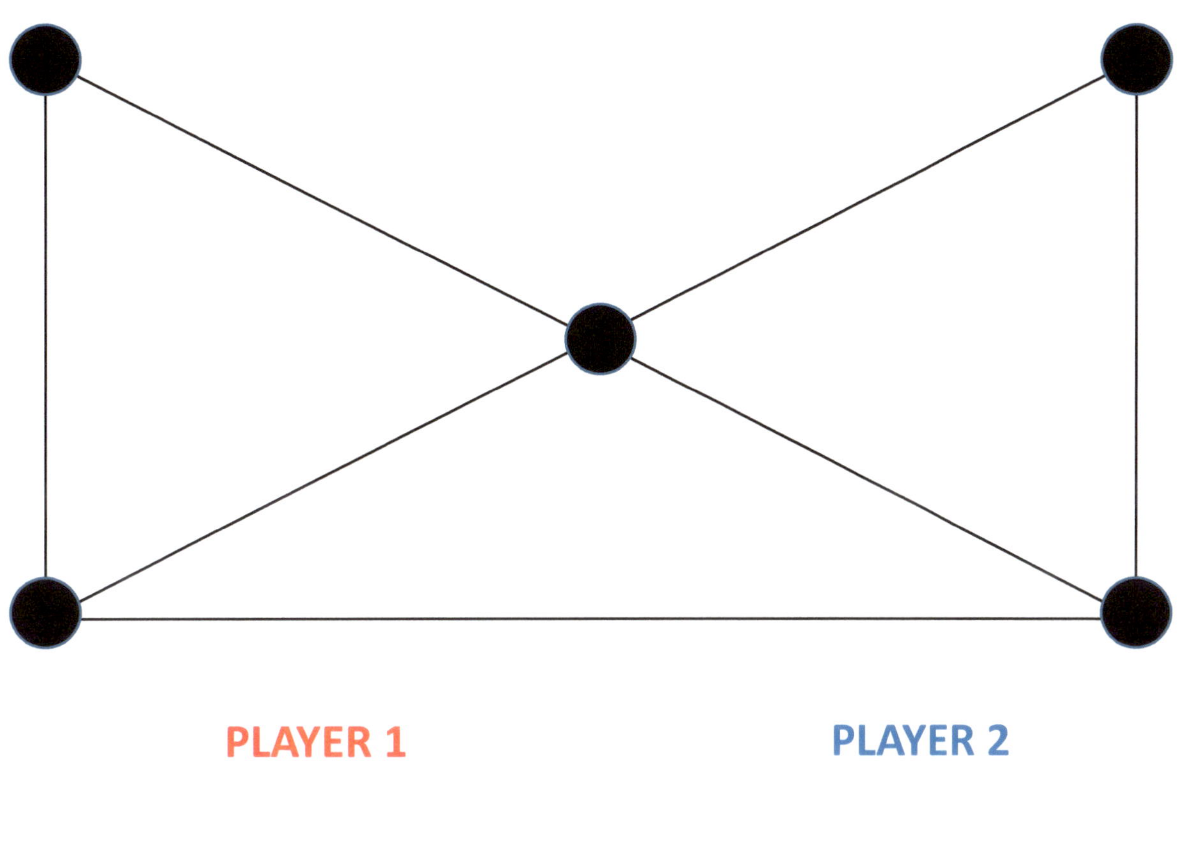

PLAYER 1   **PLAYER 2**

_______________   _______________

You can cut out the dots below to use as markers or use coins.

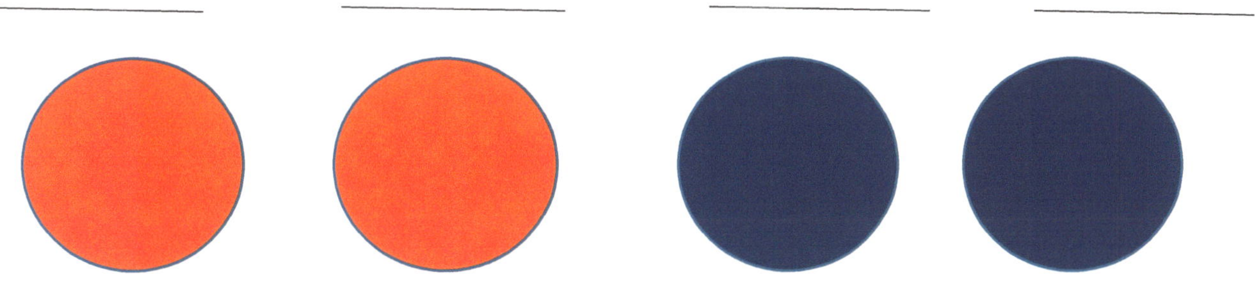

I AM THANKFUL FOR...

MOSES AND HIS STAFF

Exodus 4:2-4

TIC TAC TOE

Players: 2
One player marks X's; the other player marks O's. Take turns marking your blocks.
A player wins when they have marked 3 blocks in a row, vertically, diagonally, or horizontally.

PLAYER 1   **PLAYER 2**   **PLAYER 1**   **PLAYER 2**

PLAYER 1   **PLAYER 2**   **PLAYER 1**   **PLAYER 2**

READING FUN

BARN

HORSE

RAIN

SUN

TREE

BIRD

BINGO FUN ON THE ROAD

Players: 1 per bingo card

When you see any of the pictures below, put an X on it. The first person to have a row with 5 X's is a winner! Row may be diagonal, horizontal, or vertical.

				CHURCH
		TRUCK		BIKE
BOY	 STOP	FREE SPACE	 SPEED LIMIT 55	
				CAR
COW		GIRL	 YIELD	

BULLS & COWS

Players: 2

One player thinks of a 4-digit number (Example: 1234). The other player tries to guess it by putting a 4-digit number in the Guesses squares (one digit per square). The first player tells the second player how many bulls and cows he has guessed. Bull = correct number in the correct position (Example: 1 in the first position would be a bull). Cow = correct number in an incorrect position. Second player wins if they can guess correctly all four numbers, in correct order, before the end of the grid.

BULLS	COWS	GUESSES			

PLAYER 1

PLAYER 2

CONNECT 4 FUN

Players: 2
Each player picks a different color to color their disks. Take turns as you try to build a horizontal,
vertical, or diagonal row of 4 while preventing the other player from doing the same.
The first player to connect 4 disks wins!

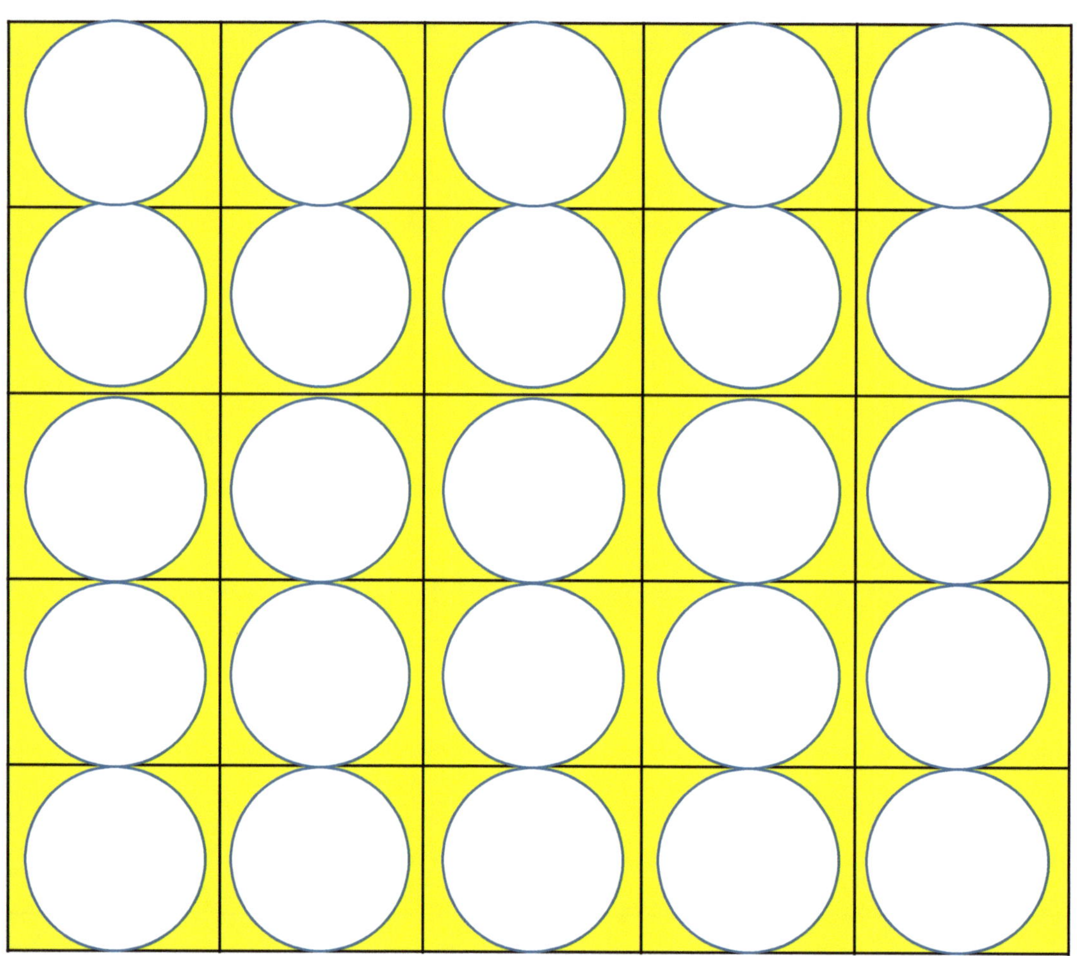

PLAYER 1   PLAYER 2

________________   ________________

John 15:12

TIC TAC TOE

Players: 2
One player marks X's; the other player marks O's. Take turns marking your blocks.
A player wins when they have marked 3 blocks in a row, vertically, diagonally, or horizontally.

PLAYER 1   **PLAYER 2**   **PLAYER 1**   **PLAYER 2**

PLAYER 1   **PLAYER 2**   **PLAYER 1**   **PLAYER 2**

ON YOUR MARKERS

Players: 2

Each player starts by putting a marker on a dot. When both players have put their two markers on two separate dots, players take turns moving their dots to the empty dot using the lines. When one player can no longer move their dot, the other player wins the game!

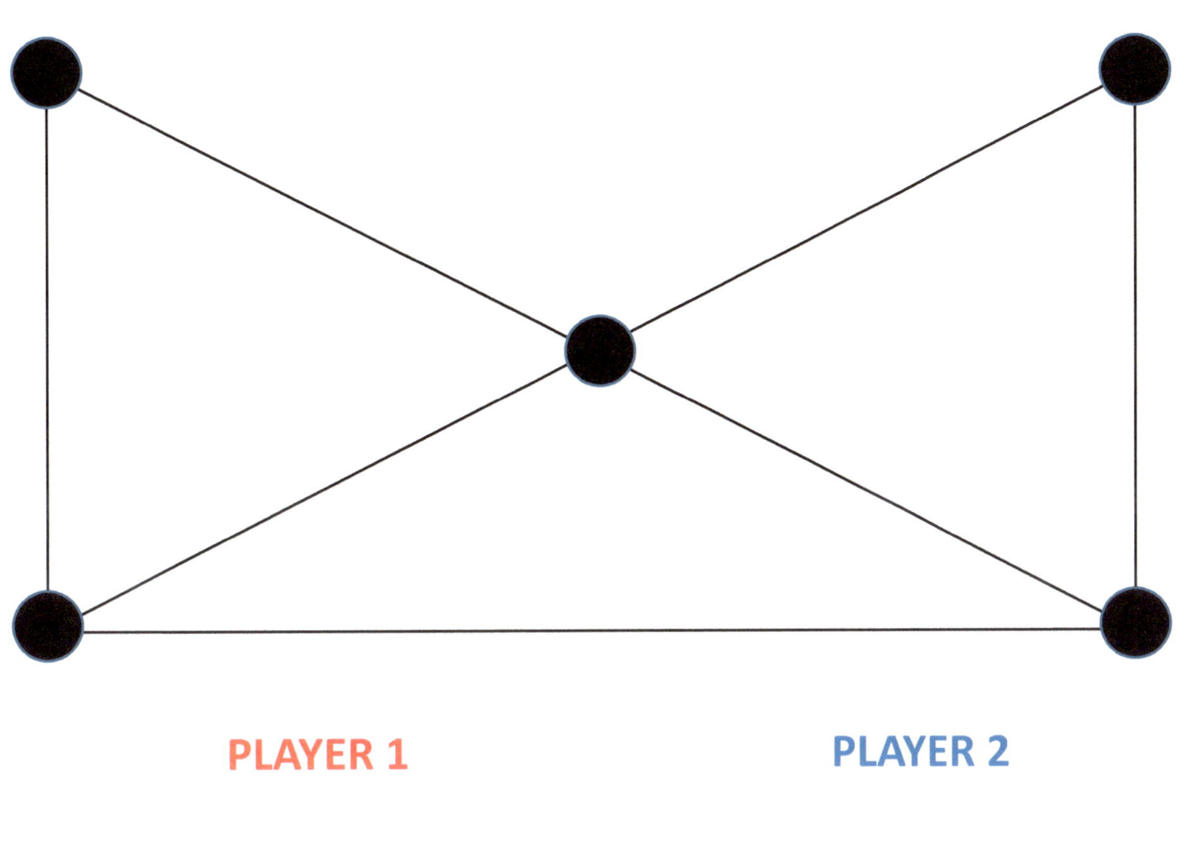

PLAYER 1 **PLAYER 2**

You can cut out the dots below to use as markers or use coins.

PICK A VERSE TO MEMORIZE!

LUKE 2:52:
AND JESUS INCREASED WITH WISDOM AND STATURE, AND IN FAVOR WITH GOD AND MAN.

JOHN 3:16:
FOR GOD SO LOVED THE WORLD THAT HE GAVE HIS ONLY BEGOTTEN SON THAT WHOSOEVER BELIEVETH IN HIM SHOULD NOT PERISH, BUT HAVE EVERLASTING LIFE.

PSALM 100:1:
MAKE A JOYFUL NOISE UNTO THE LORD, ALL YE LANDS.

GENESIS 1:1:
IN THE BEGINNING, GOD CREATED THE HEAVEN AND THE EARTH.

BINGO FUN ON THE ROAD

Players: 1 per bingo card
When you see any of the pictures below, put an X
on it. The first person to have a row with 5 X's is a
winner! Row may be diagonal, horizontal, or vertical.

BIKE	 STOP	BOY		
			GIRL	 DO NOT ENTER
TRUCK	 SCHOOL BUS / STOP	FREE SPACE		
	 YIELD	CHURCH		SCHOOL
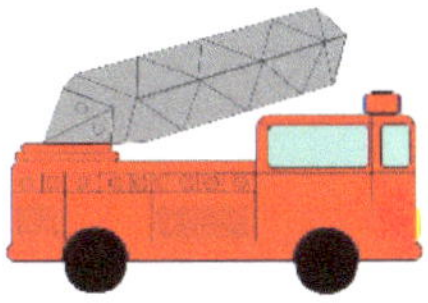	CAR		 SPEED LIMIT 55	

JESUS HEALS A MAN

John 5:8-9

CONNECT 4 FUN

Players: 2

Each player picks a different color to color their disks. Take turns as you try to build a horizontal, vertical, or diagonal row of 4 while preventing the other player from doing the same.

The first player to connect 4 disks wins!

PLAYER 1   **PLAYER 2**

_______________________   _______________________

BULLS & COWS

Players: 2

One player thinks of a 4-digit number (Example: 1234). The other player tries to guess it by putting a 4-digit number in the Guesses squares (one digit per square). The first player tells the second player how many bulls and cows he has guessed. Bull = correct number in the correct position (Example: 1 in the first position would be a bull). Cow = correct number in an incorrect position. Second player wins if they can guess correctly all four numbers, in correct order, before the end of the grid.

BULLS	COWS	GUESSES			

PLAYER 1   PLAYER 2

HELP FROM FRIENDS

Mark 2:4-5

CONNECT 4 FUN

Players: 2
Each player picks a different color to color their disks. Take turns as you try to build a horizontal,
vertical, or diagonal row of 4 while preventing the other player from doing the same.
The first player to connect 4 disks wins!

PLAYER 1   **PLAYER 2**

_______________   _______________

BLOCK 'EM FUN

Players: 2
One player marks X's; the other player marks O's. Take turns marking your blocks. You cannot mark a block next to the other player's marked block; leave at least one empty block in between.
A player wins when the other player has no block left to mark.

PLAYER 1 ________________

PLAYER 2 ________________

BINGO FUN ON THE ROAD

Players: 1 per bingo card

When you see any of the pictures below, put an X on it. The first person to have a row with 5 X's is a winner! Row may be diagonal, horizontal, or vertical.

		COW	 SPEED LIMIT 55	BOY
	CAR			TRUCK
		FREE SPACE		 YIELD
	GIRL	 STOP		SCHOOL
		BIKE	 SCHOOL BUS / STOP	

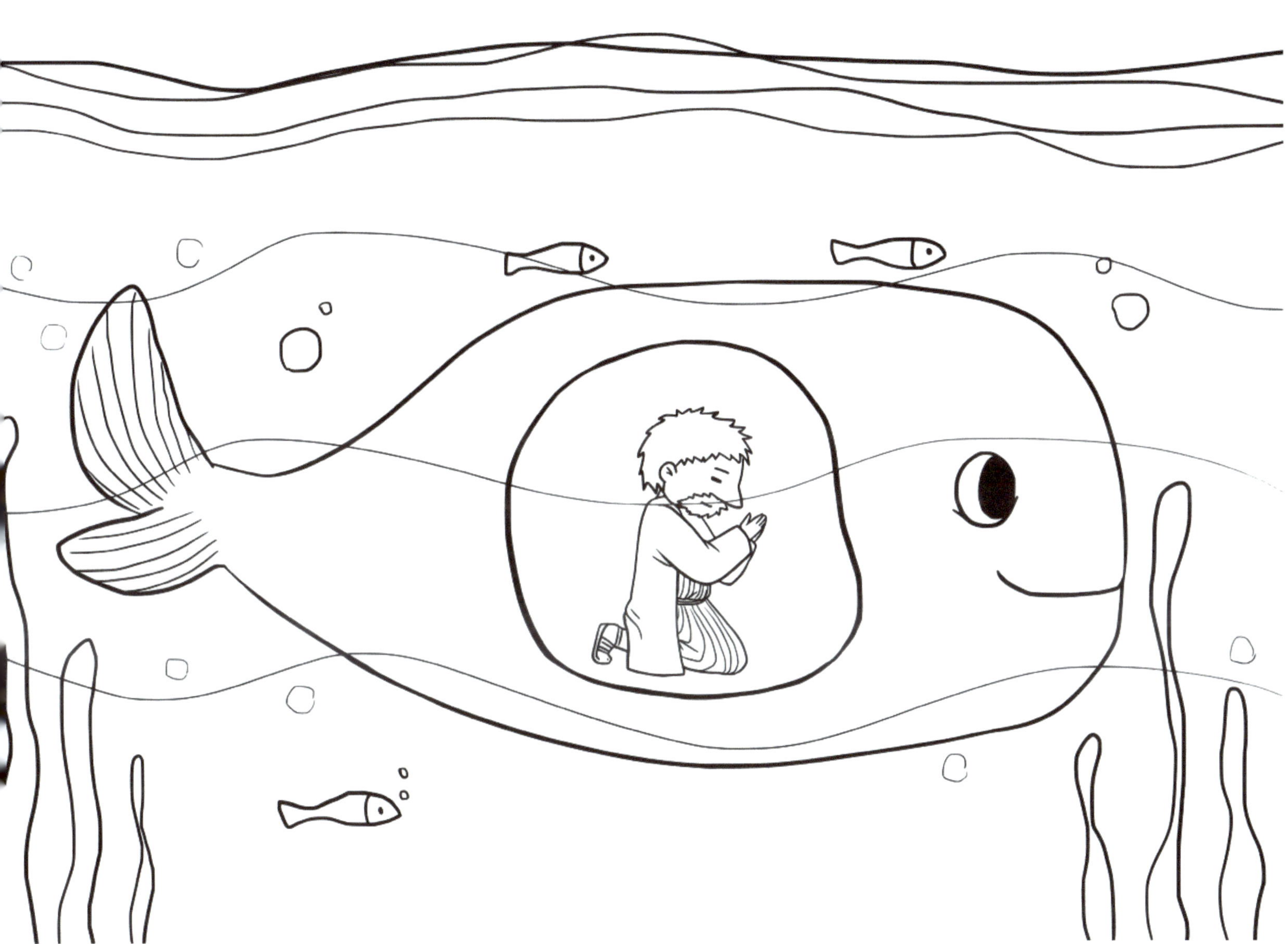

JONAH AND THE FISH

Jonah 1:17

MATCHING

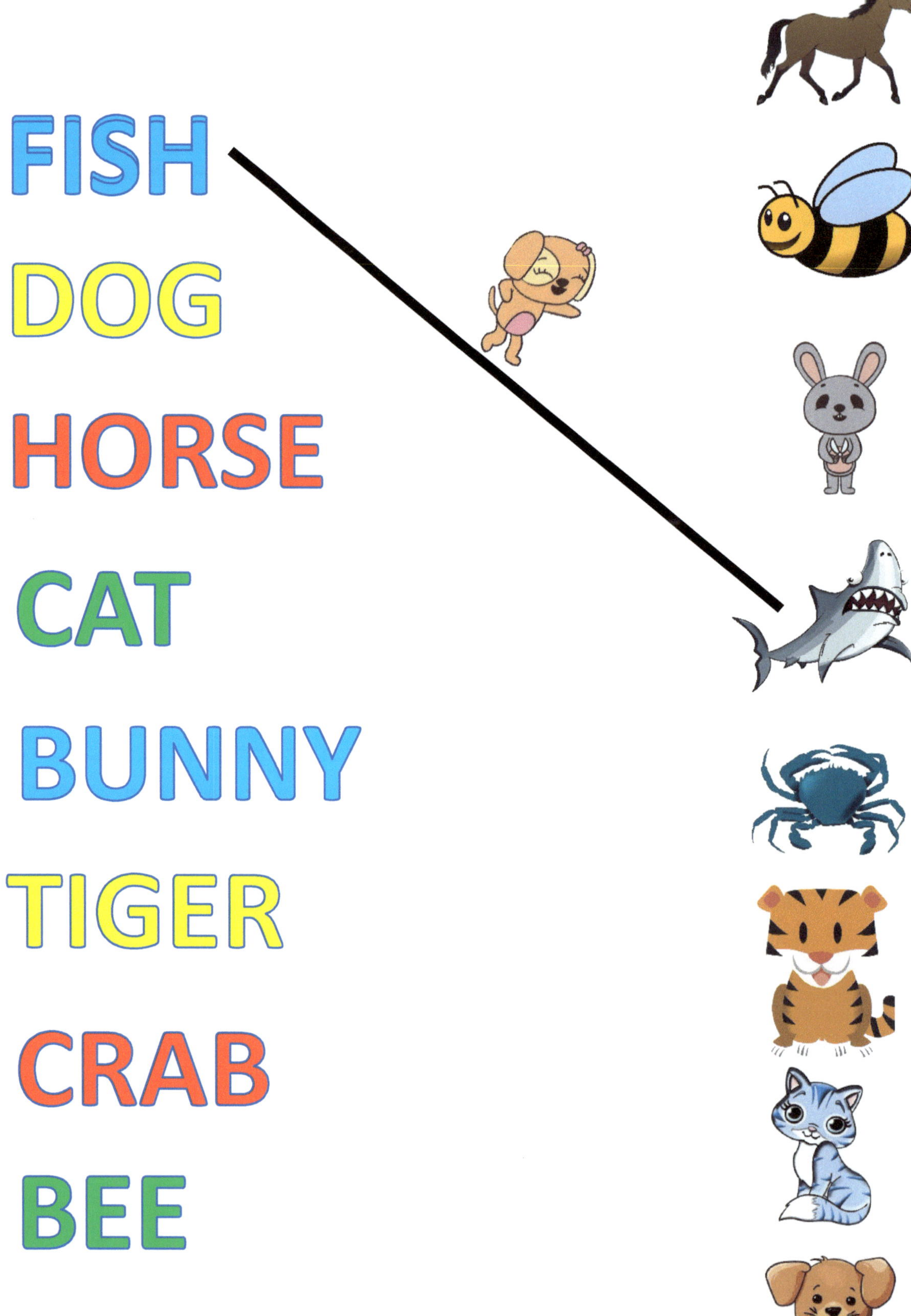

BLOCK 'EM FUN

Players: 2

One player marks X's; the other player marks O's. Take turns marking your blocks. You cannot mark a block next to the other player's marked block; leave at least one empty block in between.
A player wins when the other player has no block left to mark.

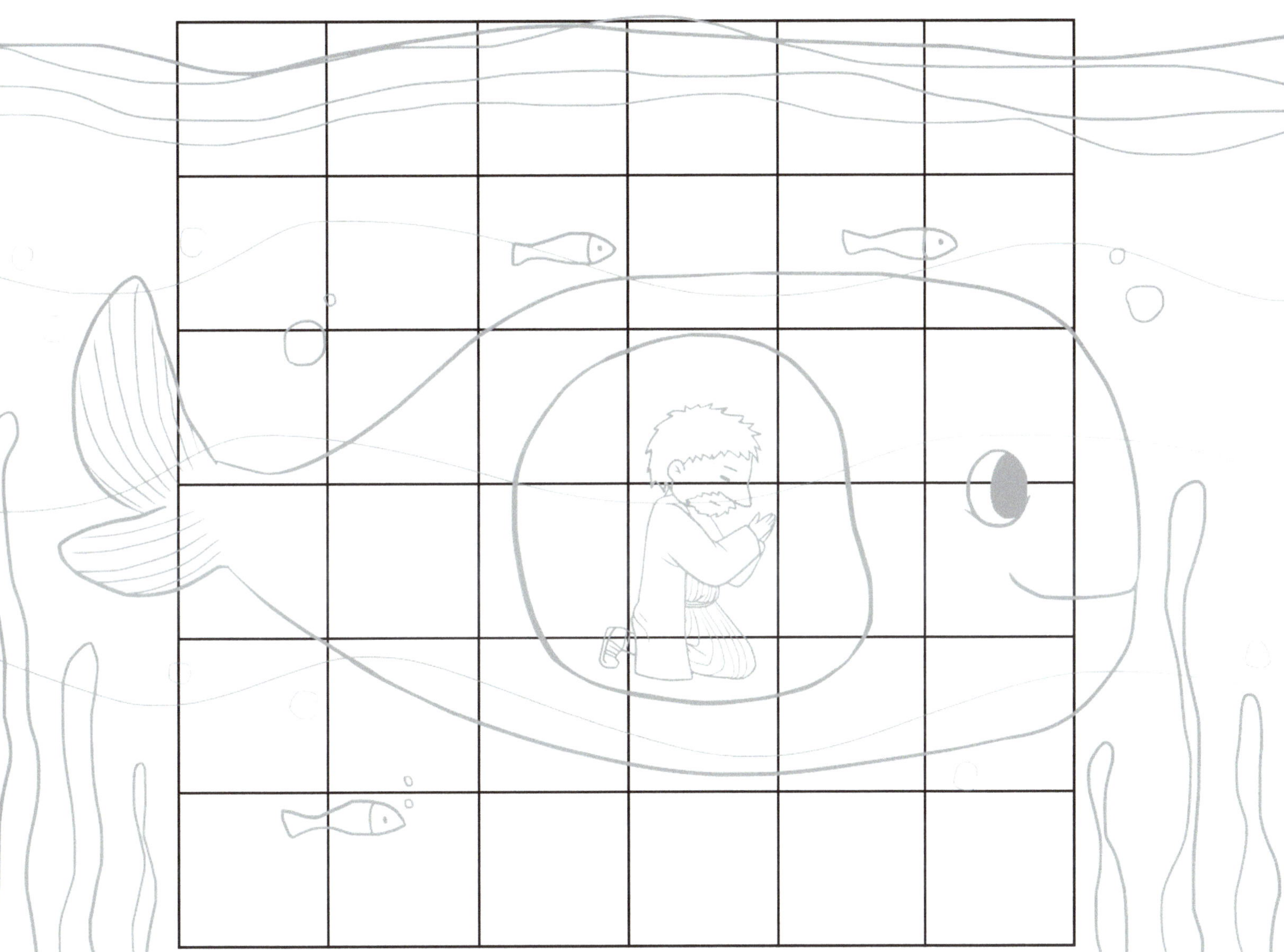

PLAYER 1

PLAYER 2

BINGO FUN ON THE ROAD

Players: 1 per bingo card

When you see any of the pictures below, put an X on it. The first person to have a row with 5 X's is a winner! Row may be diagonal, horizontal, or vertical.

	**BIKE**		**ROAD**	

CHURCH		**FREE SPACE**		**SCHOOL**
		**TRUCK**		**BOY**
	**CAR**		**GIRL**	

BLOCK 'EM FUN

Players: 2
One player marks X's; the other player marks O's. Take turns marking your blocks. You cannot mark a block next to the other player's marked block; leave at least one empty block in between.
A player wins when the other player has no block left to mark.

PLAYER 1   PLAYER 2

THE BURNING BUSH

Exodus 3:1-2

ON YOUR MARKERS

Players: 2
Each player starts by putting a marker on a dot. When both players have put their two markers on two separate dots, players take turns moving their dots to the empty dot using the lines.
When one player can no longer move their dot, the other player wins the game!

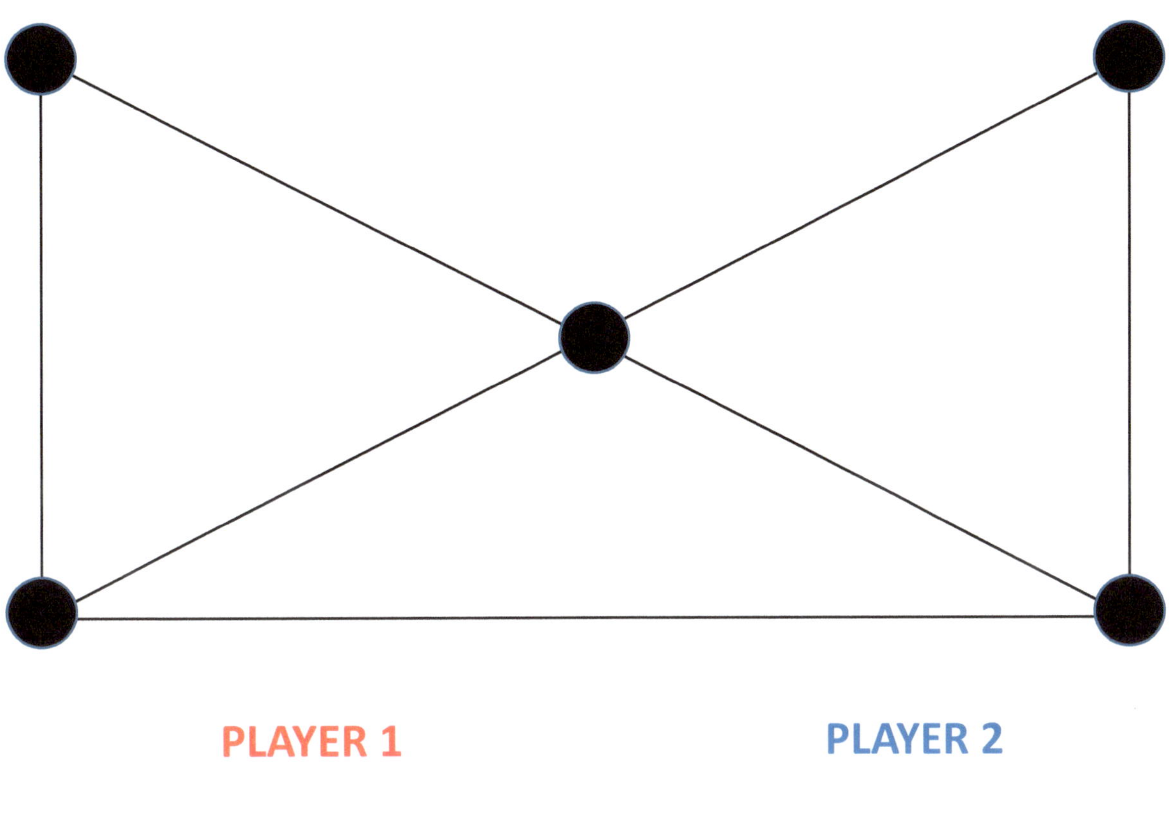

You can cut out the dots below to use as markers or use coins.

LET'S DRAW A PICTURE!

BLOCK 'EM FUN

Players: 2
One player marks X's; the other player marks O's. Take turns marking your blocks. You cannot mark a block next to the other player's marked block; leave at least one empty block in between. A player wins when the other player has no block left to mark.

PLAYER 1

PLAYER 2

BULLS & COWS

Players: 2

One player thinks of a 4-digit number (Example: 1234). The other player tries to guess it by putting a 4-digit number in the Guesses squares (one digit per square). The first player tells the second player how many bulls and cows he has guessed. Bull = correct number in the correct position (Example: 1 in the first position would be a bull). Cow = correct number in an incorrect position. Second player wins if they can guess correctly all four numbers, in correct order, before the end of the grid.

BULLS	COWS	GUESSES			

PLAYER 1   **PLAYER 2**

_______________   _______________

COLORING FUN

TIC TAC TOE

Players: 2
One player marks X's; the other player marks O's. Take turns marking your blocks.
A player wins when they have marked 3 blocks in a row, vertically, diagonally, or horizontally.

PLAYER 1 **PLAYER 2** **PLAYER 1** **PLAYER 2**

PLAYER 1 **PLAYER 2** **PLAYER 1** **PLAYER 2**

LET'S MAKE WORDS

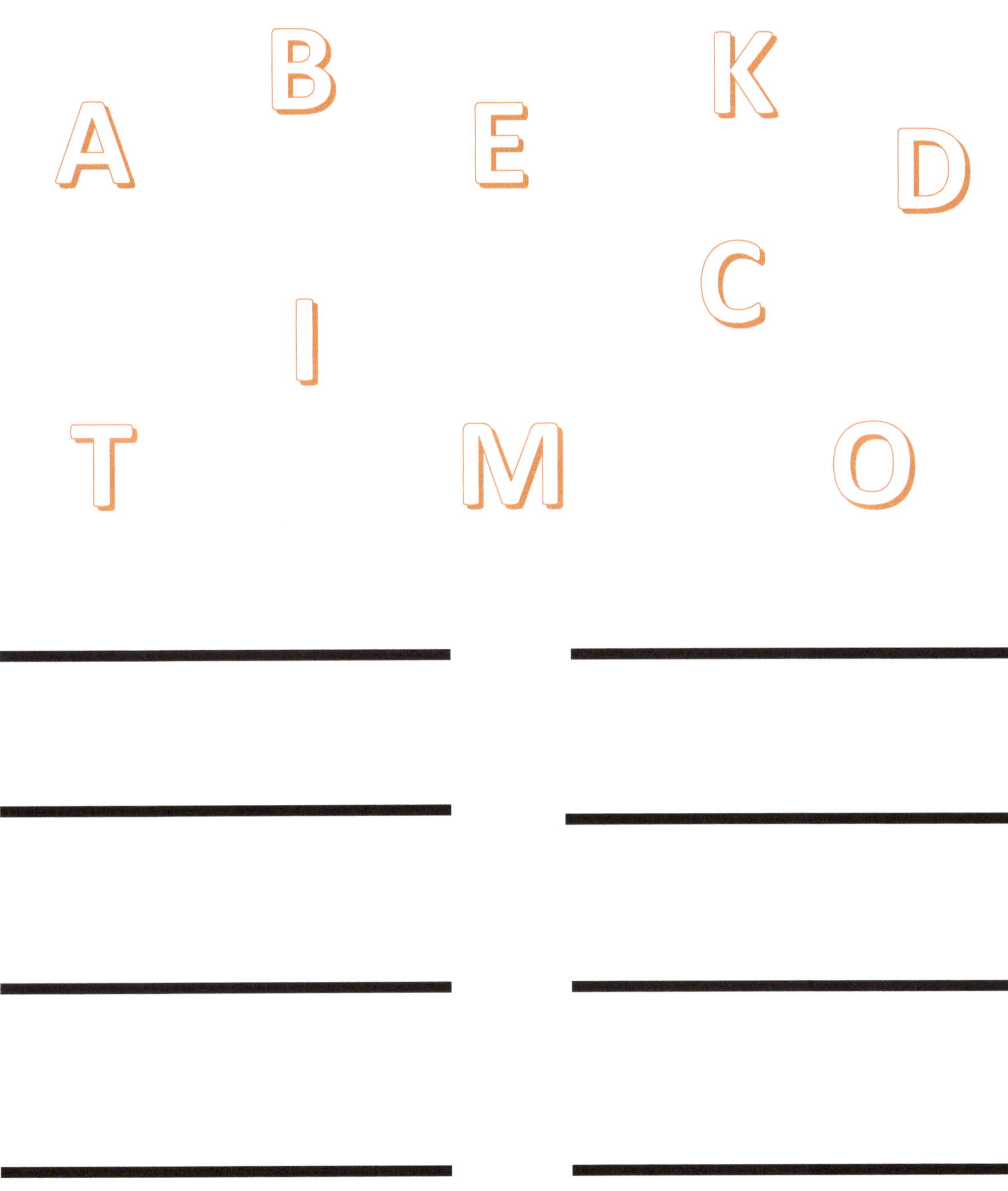

TIC TAC TOE

Players: 2
One player marks X's; the other player marks O's. Take turns marking your blocks.
A player wins when they have marked 3 blocks in a row, vertically, diagonally, or horizontally.

PLAYER 1   **PLAYER 2**   **PLAYER 1**   **PLAYER 2**

PLAYER 1   **PLAYER 2**   **PLAYER 1**   **PLAYER 2**

CONNECT 4 FUN

Players: 2
Each player picks a different color to color their disks. Take turns as you try to build a horizontal,
vertical, or diagonal row of 4 while preventing the other player from doing the same.
The first player to connect 4 disks wins!

PLAYER 1　　　　　　　**PLAYER 2**

__________________　　　　__________________

TIC TAC TOE

Players: 2
One player marks X's; the other player marks O's. Take turns marking your blocks.
A player wins when they have marked 3 blocks in a row, vertically, diagonally, or horizontally.

PLAYER 1   PLAYER 2   PLAYER 1   PLAYER 2

PLAYER 1   PLAYER 2   PLAYER 1   PLAYER 2

ON YOUR MARKERS

Players: 2

Each player starts by putting a marker on a dot. When both players have put their two markers on two separate dots, players take turns moving their dots to the empty dot using the lines.
When one player can no longer move their dot, the other player wins the game!

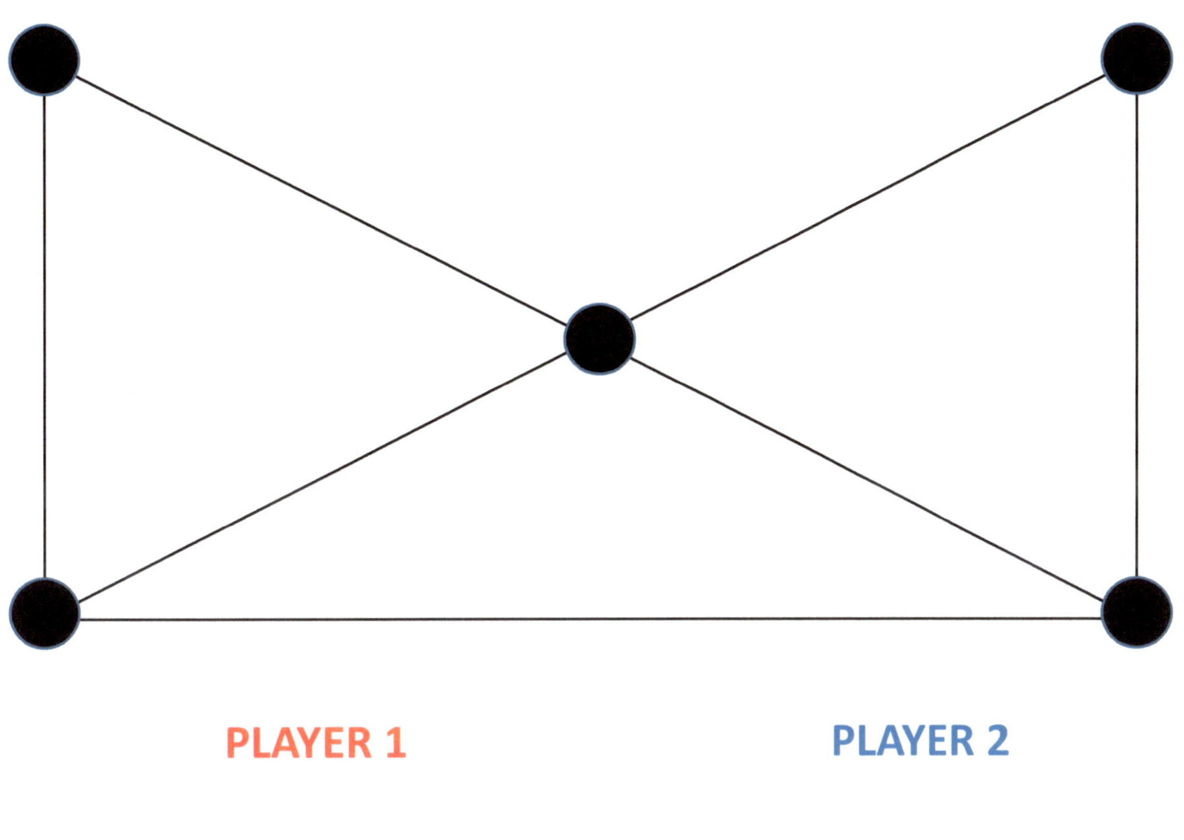

PLAYER 1   PLAYER 2

_______________   _______________

You can cut out the dots below to use as markers or use coins.

I LOVE GOD BECAUSE...

BULLS & COWS

Players: 2

One player thinks of a 4-digit number (Example: 1234). The other player tries to guess it by putting a 4-digit number in the Guesses squares (one digit per square). The first player tells the second player how many bulls and cows he has guessed. Bull = correct number in the correct position (Example: 1 in the first position would be a bull). Cow = correct number in an incorrect position. Second player wins if they can guess correctly all four numbers, in correct order, before the end of the grid.

BULLS	COWS	GUESSES			

PLAYER 1　　　　　　　　　　　　PLAYER 2

__________________　　　　　　__________________

Look for more

puzzle books and

picture books

by

JB Robor

Want laminated pages from this book?

These are especially fun and reusable, particularly for *Bingo Fun on the Road* cards!

Order from the author's website.

www.ingramcontent.com/pod-product-compliance
Lightning Source LLC
Chambersburg PA
CBHW042045110726

48006CB00002B/296